Getting There

A Transportation Dictionary

Gary Miller

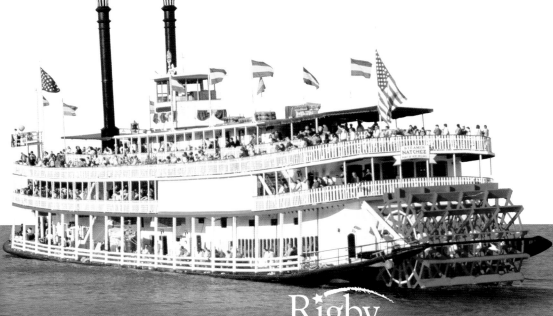

Rigby®

A Harcourt Achieve Imprint

www.Rigby.com
1-800-531-5015

Did you know that the wheel is one of the world's oldest and greatest inventions? Wheels were invented to help people go places, and people have been using the wheel to help them get around ever since!

Transportation is the act of moving people, goods, and information from place to place. This dictionary explains how transportation has changed over time.

Early artists understood the importance of wheels.

The first wheels that were used for transportation can be traced back more than 5,000 years to 3200 B.C.

Airplane

In 1903 two brothers named Orville and Wilbur Wright made history by building and flying in the first airplane. Their invention changed the world forever.

The first airplanes were small and slow, and they often crashed. But during the 1930s, people began to build better airplanes. By the 1950s, travelers were able to fly across the United States.

In 1979 Bryan Allen flew the *Gossamer Albatross* by using bicycle pedals! In 2006 Steve Fossett broke the world record by make the longest nonstop flight ever.

A human "engine" powered the *Gossamer Albatross* in 1979.

1903 The Wright brothers take the first airplane flight.

1939 The first jet airplane flies.

2006 Steve Fossett flies nonstop for 26,389 miles.

1750 1775 1800 1825 1850 1875 1900 1925 1950 1975 2000 2025

1950s People begin to fly more and more often.

1979 The *Gossamer Albatross* flies using pedal power.

...ight by the *Wright Flyer* lasted ... but it changed the world.

5

Automobile

Nicolas Cugnot of France invented the first automobile. It ran on steam power. Since his success in 1769, many inventors have built automobiles. For example, Henry Ford built the Ford Model T. Ford's car was also called the Tin Lizzy.

Today, most automobiles run on gasoline. But many carmakers are turning to electric power because gasoline creates a lot of pollution. In 1999 carmakers began selling hybrid cars to help protect the planet. A hybrid automobile runs on both gasoline and electricity.

Cugnot's steam engine is said to be the first self-powered automobile.

1769 Nicolas Cugnot builds the first automobile that runs on steam power.

1908 Henry Ford makes his first Model T.

1927 Over 18 million Model Ts have been built!

1750 1775 1800 1825 1850 1875 1900 1925 1950 1975 2000 2025

1830s The first electric automobile is built.

1999 The first car that runs on both gasoline and electricity is made.

The Ford Model T was a popular car that people liked to drive.

Bicycle

The first bicycle was called a hobbyhorse, and it didn't have pedals. Riders moved by running along the ground with their feet. The first bicycle with pedals was called a boneshaker because it was very uncomfortable to ride.

Most people today drive cars to get around, but in the last decade, bicycle riding has become popular again. Bike racers like Lance Armstrong have encouraged many Americans to ride bikes for fun, exercise, and transportation.

Today's racing bikes are very lightweight.

1860s The boneshaker bicycle arrives in Connecticut.

2005 Lance Armstrong wins his 7th Tour de France bike race.

1920s Most Americans drive cars instead of riding bikes.

1974 Americans buy 14 million bicycles.

1750 1775 1800 1825 1850 1875 1900 1925 1950 1975 2000 2025

This bike from the 1860s was called a boneshaker.

Steamboat

Before airplanes and automobiles were invented, people used boats for travel. The first boats powered by steam were invented in the late 1700s. They traveled 5 miles per hour. In 1807 Robert Fulton built the *Clermont*, the first steamboat to successfully travel 40 miles in 8 hours. This boat could carry over 100 people.

Steamboat travel wasn't always enjoyable. The boats sometimes hit underwater objects and sank. Steam engines often exploded. Newer inventions took the place of steamboats by the 1870s, but a few steamboats still travel the Mississippi River.

People still take steamboat rides on the Mississippi River for fun.

1807 Robert Fulton builds the *Clermont*.

1870s Newer transportation begins to take the place of steamboats.

1750　1775　1800　1825　1850　1875　1900　1925　1950　1975　2000　2025

Steamboats like this were once a common sight.

Subway

Built like a train with many cars, a subway carries passengers underground. People ride subways to work, to school, and to visit friends. Without subways, cities would be even more jammed with automobiles.

The first subway ran in London, England, in 1863. In 1897 America's first subway opened for business in Boston, Massachusetts. By 1904 New York City had finished its subway, which now has 463 subway stations, the most in the world!

During busy times, finding a seat on a subway car isn't always easy.

1863 The first subway opens in London, England.

1904 The New York City subway begins running.

1750 1775 1800 1825 1850 1875 1900 1925 1950 1975 2000 2025

1897 Boston opens the first subway in the United States.

Workers spent years digging tunnels for the New York City subway.

Train

Did you know that the first trains were pulled by horses? In 1804 Richard Trevithick invented the first steam engine that pulled train cars. By 1830 the first American steam train began running. George Pullman invented the Pullman Sleeping Car in 1857 so that people could travel on trains at night.

Trains were the fastest way to transport people and cargo until the 1900s. Then Americans began using cars and trucks for work and travel. However, millions of Americans still travel on passenger trains today.

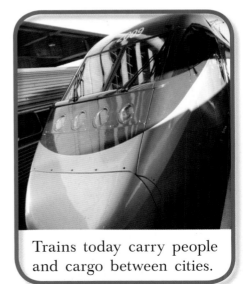

Trains today carry people and cargo between cities.

1804 Richard Trevithick builds the first steam train.

1857 George Pullman invents the Pullman Sleeping Car.

1750 1775 1800 1825 1850 1875 1900 1925 1950 1975 2000 2025

1830 The first American trains begin running.

2004 The United States has 121,400 miles of railroad track.

This steam-driven engine pulled early train cars.

Transportation moves more than people and cargo. It also moves information. And to do that, we don't need to move at all! Students worldwide can work on a project together through video technology or use information over the Internet.

How can transportation improve our lives in the future? Can you think of better ways to move people, things, and information?